ODETTA
THE QUEEN OF FOLK

POEM BY SAMANTHA THORNHILL

CONCEIVED AND ILLUSTRATED BY
STEPHEN ALCORN

SCHOLASTIC PRESS
NEW YORK

This is the story
of a girl
who plunged
headfirst
into the world,
a baby with a birdcage
in her throat.

What to name
this little ball
of star stuff
        and song
        and light
straight from God's eye?

Odetta.
The perfect name
for a star this brown
and this bright!

Someone in Birmingham, Alabama, a long long time ago must've accidentally burned the Christmas ham. That's how the city of Birmingham got its nickname — Burning Ham.

Burning Ham
is where baby Odetta
plunged into the world
and grew
        and grew
into a shy little
lamb of a girl.
Timid as she was,
Odetta loved
making a whole
heap of noise
with the help
of Auntie's piano.

In little Odetta's
imagination, she was
a wildly famous musician
playing for a sea of her
folk, Mama clapping
from the front row.

But to poor Auntie,
little Odetta had a special talent
for making that piano
sound like a circus
of pots and pans
hurtling straight
outta heaven!

Or a midnight train
railroading right
through her living room.

So the saying goes:
One soul's noise
is another soul's music.

Now, Auntie loved her
niece and all, but not
as much as she hated
those headaches her piano
playing caused.

So little Odetta
had no choice but
to shut
the lid
on all
those pretty keys,
zip the lip
on her great big dreams
that she could make
black keys
        and white keys
work together
to create AWESOME
sound.

'Cause in the Deep
South, 'round Odetta's
parts, black
        and white
didn't mix so well,
and when they did
it was mighty gray
with a whole lot
of noise—not music—
NOISE!

Sometimes things
could be downright
depressing.

Folk bending
their backs
in cotton fields
from can't see
          to can't see,
spirituals blooming
from split lips.

Prison men
on the chain gang dressed
in stripes
        and chains
singing songs
        like slaves
working together
        like keys
to create beautiful
        and furious
prison songs!

Spirituals, gospel,
prison, and work
songs: the cup
of soup Odetta
grew up on!

*Songs of joys
and sorrows,
songs of rivers
and sparrows.*

Sorrow songs sung
by the miracle,
Marian Anderson.

Tunes composed
by "cotton picking"
Greats.

Melodies peppered
with the "UH" and "AH"
of backbreaking work.

Times were crazy!
Back then, this cat
named Jim Crow was so
popular, kids Odetta's age
must've thought
he was president.

He had signs above every
fountain in Burning Ham,
saying, "Whites Only"
and "For Coloreds."

These signs made
Odetta look down.
Were there fountains
for her and her mama?
It made Odetta feel
not quite right.
She and Mama weren't
white
        or colored,
just like the world wasn't
up
        or down.
She and Mama
were BROWN!

One day, Mama
announced they were moving
to *Lost* Angeles,
California, some place
way on the other
side of daylight.

Six-year-old Odetta never
heard of this place
in all her little life.
Took her six tries
to say it right.
      Los Angeles.

The day they boarded
the train to California
was one Odetta
would never forget.
'Twas the day she met
President Jim
Crow himself.

His eyes were glacier
blue, his hair
the color of smoke.
Seemed he came
all the way from
White House Land
just to tell Odetta's folk
they had gone too far.

They were sitting in the
WRONG TRAIN CAR!

Everyone watched
Odetta's folk load
their lives up
in their arms
and exit the car
dang near tiptoe
all 'cause Jim Crow
SAID SO!

Odetta's little fists
clenched,
        then unfurled.
What could she do?
After all, she was just
a scared brown girl in this
grown-up
        messed-up
world.

This little
girl from Burning Ham, Alabama,
had no song
to sing, no pot
to stir her sorrows in.

The birdcage
in her throat imprisoned
her bird, its door
tightly hinged.

Good riddance, Burning Ham!

From the cramped
Jim Crow car,
from the cramped
Knee grow car.

In Los Angeles,
city of steeples,
there was only one
sort of water
fountain, the kind
for thirsty people.

*City of wings
and haloes,
city of hawks
and sparrows.*

When Odetta grew
good and tall,
she understood Jim Crow
wasn't a man at all,
but a bunch
of silly laws that
made black folks
pause and feel
bad
about themselves.

J. Crow had no
heart, no lungs.
Just daughters
and sons.

Mama could finally
afford Odetta some
piano lessons once
she became a teen.
Remember all
those pretty keys
shining
like Afro Sheen?

Odetta peeled back
that lid still
determined to make
black keys
        and white keys
work together
to create SENSATIONAL sound.

Odetta found
freedom by
accident
the day
she opened
her mouth,
then closed
her eyes
and sang.
For once
she saw
no color.
That's when
she shook
hands with
Harmony!

The birdcage
in her throat
grew too small
for her bird,
and its door
unhinged.

There it goes!

There goes Odetta
again with that bird
in her throat,
the way it flew
out her mouth
and soared high,
higher than angels fly!

And how she loved
to make that bird
fly high, then dip low.
The way Odetta sang,
not even Jim Crow
could tell her no!

Odetta sang
        and sang,
making that bird soar
higher
        and higher,
its feathers
sparkling in the sun
and glistening
with God's tears.

Odetta couldn't
just *sing*, she
could *sang*.
To *sang* is to sing
like you need the music
as much
        as birds
        need sky.

Have you ever
heard a song
come from deep
in the knees?
You ever heard
her Baby cry?

Baby: Odetta's guitar,
pure heaven clothed
in wood,
          strings,
          silence.

Named Baby
'cause it weighed a ton.
Named Baby
'cause she held it like
one.

There's the prince
of pop and the king
of rock and roll,
but they're the egg whites . . .
so who's the yolk?

Odetta, Queen of Folk!

Folk music,
bulldozer
of sound:
the tunes
that paved
the way
CREATED
the fray
and make
you cry
like pepper
spray.

Watch poets pick up
guitars, bob
their heads, and pick
their fingers numb
just to echo that
Odetta strum.

Watch women
kink up their hair,
look in their mirrors,
and feel better.
Watch women
rocking the 'fro known
as "the Odetta"!

Millions
have huddled to hear
her sing in the sun,
wind, and rain.

Dogs and night,
sticks and hoses, oh
my!
She brings us beauty.
She brings the pain.

She croons
the rich stuff
that oozed
out the poor
folk who didn't
doze but BULLdozed
our paths
to greatness.

The microphone
        her throne
"the Odetta,"
        her crown.
When the Queen
of Folk closes her eyes
and sings hard,
she travels all
the way back
down
to the swamps,
the cotton fields,
the chain gang,
the church, to
Jim Crow SAID SO, to
"heck no, we won't go,"
to her very first
memories, spirituals
and melodies peppered
with the "UH!"
        and "AH!"
of backbreaking work.

Odetta been carrying
these songs all
along, those tunes
from waaay back,
filling the endless cotton
sack of her musical memory.

The walls of sold out
concert halls leak tunes
that grow out of Odetta's
soul like a new bruise:
the blacks
        and the blues.

*Songs of rivers
and sparrows,
songs of joys
and sorrows.*

Now, we may not all
sing the same, but we
can all sing along.
Let's sing with the Queen
of Folk, this wildly
famous song:

This little light of mine.
I'm gonna let it shine.

Black keys
        and white keys
singing TOGETHER
to create HARMONIOUS sound!

ODE TO ODETTA

One of the brightest stars of the early 1960s folk music renaissance, Odetta Holmes was born in Birmingham, Alabama, on December 31, 1930. Although classically trained, she found herself drawn to the warmth, dignity, and tenderness of early African-American spirituals, and by the mid 1950s had become inextricably linked to the folk circuit, touring extensively in the United States and Canada. By 1961, she had played Carnegie Hall and appeared twice at the renowned Newport Folk Festival. In the process, she developed the sound canonized in the folk music world as "the Odetta strum"—a distinctive rhythm often played on a large, bulbous guitar (a rhythm embellished by intriguing chordal modifications and bold, lyrical flourishes). In time, her name became synonymous not only with her guitar playing but with the guitar itself. This instrument was an extension of her heart, voice, and soul for more than sixty years.

Odetta's influence on younger folk singers is legendary. She provided inspiration to Joan Baez, Janis Joplin, and Joan Armatrading. And, more famously, Odetta is the one Bob Dylan credits for his decision (made while still a teenager) to trade in his electric guitar for an acoustic one, thus heralding his entry into the realm of folk music. In turn, Odetta would draw inspiration from the post–Civil War Jubilee Singers' tradition (carried on in the twentieth century by Marian Anderson, Roland Hayes, and Paul Robeson), from the ethnic field recordings of Leadbelly, Vera Hall, and Dock Reed, as well as from rural and urban blues, work, and protest songs, modern and traditional jazz, classical, and opera.

A woman of wide-ranging political interests, Odetta participated in the 1963 and 1983 marches on

Washington and the Selma to Montgomery civil rights march in 1965. She lobbied under the auspices of the American Arts Alliance and co-chaired the fifteenth anniversary of the National Association for Working Women. For her contributions to numerous humanitarian organizations and causes, she received the Lifetime Achievement Award of the World Folk Music Association. In 1987, the National Music Council presented her with its American Eagle Award for her distinguished contribution to American music.

Odetta died in 2008, leaving behind a legacy of music that will endure forever.   —STEPHEN ALCORN

Photograph by Sabina Alcorn

Odetta and Stephen Alcorn

In a recording career that spanned fifty-four years, Odetta left her unique personal stamp on a wide range of musical idioms, most notably American folk, blues, jazz, and spirituals. The following selection of recordings is tailored to showcase the remarkable breadth and scope of her repertoire.

Odetta Sings Ballads and Blues Tradition Records (1956)
Odetta and The Blues Riverside/Original Blues Classics (1962)
Odetta Sings Dylan RCA Records (1965)

Blues Everywhere I Go M.C. Records (1999)
Looking For A Home (A Tribute to Huddie Ledbetter, aka Leadbelly) M.C. Records (2001)
Gonna Let It Shine: A Concert for the Holidays M.C. Records (2005)

Compilations:
The Essential Odetta Vanguard (1973)
Odetta: Absolutely the Best Fuel (2000)

For my mother, to whom I owe the
omnipresent joy of music in my life.
                                    —S.A.

ACKNOWLEDGMENTS
This book was made possible by the trust, generosity, and gracious
cooperation of Odetta, my heroine; and by the steadfast support and
dedication of Sabina, my wife and muse.

Special thanks to Jonathan Hiam, Head, American Music Collection,
the New York Public Library for the Performing Arts, for consulting
on this book.

Library of Congress Cataloging-in-Publication Data Available
ISBN 978-0-439-92818-2

10 9 8 7 6 5 4 3 2 1   10 11 12 13 14

Printed in Singapore   46
First edition, December 2010

The text was set in Adobe Garamond Pro Regular.
The display type was set in Davida BT.
The illustrations were done in casein paint on paper.
Art direction and book design by Marijka Kostiw